Autumn Story

Jill Barklem

TED SMART

For David

This edition specially produced in 1997 for The Book People Ltd,
Catteshall Manor, Catteshall Lane,
Godalming, SURREY GU7 1UU

First edition published in Great Britain by
HarperCollins Publishers Ltd in 1980
Reprinted twenty-nine times
New edition 1995
2 4 6 8 10 9 7 5 3 1

A CIP catalogue record for this title is available
from the British Library.

ISBN 0-583-33325-7

Printed and bound in Singapore

BRAMBLY HEDGE

For many generations, families of mice have made their homes in the roots and trunks of the trees of Brambly Hedge, a dense and tangled hedgerow that borders the field on the other side of the stream.

The Brambly Hedge mice lead busy lives. During the fine weather, they collect flowers, fruits, berries and nuts from the Hedge and surrounding fields, and prepare delicious jams, pickles and preserves that are kept safely in the Store Stump for the winter months ahead.

Although the mice work hard, they make time for fun too. All through the year, they mark the seasons with feasts and festivities and, whether it be a little mouse's birthday, an eagerly awaited wedding or the first day of spring, the mice welcome the opportunity to meet and celebrate.

It was a fine autumn. The blackberries were ripe and the nuts were ready, and the mice of Brambly Hedge were very busy. Every morning they went out into the fields to gather seeds, berries and roots, which they took back to the Store Stump and carefully stowed away for the winter ahead. The Store Stump was warm inside and smelled deliciously of bramble jelly and rising bread, and it was already nearly full of food.

Lord Woodmouse, who lived in the Old Oak Palace, was out early with his youngest daughter, Primrose.

"Now keep close to me and don't get lost," he said, as they made their way along the blackberry bushes. Primrose picked the berries nearest the ground while her father hooked the upper branches down with his walking stick.

The basket was nearly full when they were joined by old Mrs Eyebright.

"I've been looking for you," she said. "Bad weather's on its way, I can feel it in my bones. We must finish our harvesting before the rain begins."

Lord Woodmouse sent Primrose back to the Palace and then went on to the Store Stump to find Mr Apple to make arrangements. Soon parties of mice with carts and wheelbarrows were hurrying out to the fields to gather the last of the nuts and berries.

Lord and Lady Woodmouse decided to help pick mushrooms and they were just setting off when Lady Woodmouse cried out in alarm, "Where's Primrose?"

She was nowhere to be seen.

She wasn't hiding in the baskets, or under the leaves, or in the long grass.

"Has anyone seen Primrose?" shouted Lord Woodmouse.

"She hasn't been here," replied the mice gathering berries high in the blackthorn bush.

"We haven't seen her," called the mice in the tangly hawthorn trees.

The children thought she was at her grandmother's house and a search party was sent along to investigate.

Hot and out of breath, they knocked at the door of Crabapple Cottage.

"Have you seen Primrose?" asked Wilfred. "We've lost her."

Mrs Apple shook her head, took off her apron, and joined in the search. Mr Apple ran over to the gap in the hedge by the Store Stump.

"Primrose, where are you?" he cried.

"Primrose, where are you?" echoed the call across the cornfield.

Lord and Lady Woodmouse went back to the Palace. They looked in the cupboards and under the beds. The Store Stump was searched from top to bottom.

"Oh dear!" said Lady Daisy. "She's such a little mouse. Where can she be? What shall we do?"

Meanwhile, Primrose, wandering along the edge of the cornfield, was quite unaware of her parents' concern. She had spent the morning picking wild flowers and gazing up at the blue sky, and after a lunch of blackberries, she had dozed a little in the sun. She was just going to help a group of mice she had seen gathering seeds in the ditch, when she spotted a little round house high up in the stalks of the corn.

"I wonder who lives there," she thought, and decided to climb up and peep through one of the windows.

As she looked in, she saw two pairs of bright little eyes peering back at her.

"I–I do beg your pardon," she stammered, and began to climb down again.

"We were just going to have tea," a voice called after her, "won't you join us?"

Primrose found the tiny front door and went inside. It was very cosy. There was a thistledown carpet on the floor and the neatly-woven grass walls were covered with books and pictures. The two elderly harvest mice who lived in the house were very glad to have a visitor. They sat Primrose down, gave her a slice of cake and handed her their album of family portraits to look at.

When Primrose had been shown all their treasures, she thanked the mice politely and climbed down to the ground again. She decided to walk to the edge of the Chestnut Woods before she went home. Some Brambly Hedge mice were still there, picking blackberries in the last of the evening sun, but they were too busy to notice her. She peered into the grasses, looking for feathers and other useful things.

Hidden in the brambles, she discovered a very interesting hole.

"I wonder if anyone lives down there," she said to herself and wandered into the tunnel.

It was very dark inside but she could just see round front doors set in the walls of the branching passages. As she went deeper into the tunnel it became darker still and soon Primrose could see nothing at all.

"I don't think I like this place," said Primrose with a shiver, "I'm going home."

She turned to leave, but with so many passages leading this way and that, she had no idea which way she had come. She picked up her skirts and ran through the maze of tunnels.

At last she saw a glimmer of light and ran towards it. The passage opened into a thick clump of brambles and briars under some tall trees. Primrose had no idea where she was.

"I can't see the oak tree," she said in a small voice, "and I can't see the willow by the stream. I think I must be lost."

It was getting very dark. Big drops of rain began to fall and splashed through the leaves around her. Primrose huddled under a toadstool and tried not to cry.

In the distance a lonely owl hooted and the branches of the trees above creaked in the rising wind. There were little scrabbling noises in the bush quite near to Primrose and these worried her most of all.

It got darker and darker and soon everything disappeared into the night.

Primrose was just trying not to think about weasels, when to her horror she saw five little flickering lights coming through the woods towards her. She could just make out five strange

figures behind them. They were shapeless and bulgy and seemed to have no heads at all. Primrose wriggled further back into the brambles.

The figures came closer and closer and Primrose realised that they were going to pass right by her hiding place.

The nearer they came, the worse they looked, and she shut her eyes as she heard them pass only a whisker away from where she was sitting. One. . . two. . . three. . . four. . .

She decided to be very brave and take a peep at the fifth as it went by.

It walked with a limp. It had a tail. And whiskers. And Mr Apple's trousers.

"GRANDPA!" she squeaked with delight.

As each of the figures turned round she recognised them; Mr Apple, Mrs Apple, Dusty Dogwood and best of all, her own mother and father.

Primrose pushed her way through the brambles.

"Primrose!" cried Lady Daisy. "You're safe!"

"The harvest mice said you had gone to the woods, but it was so dark and wet that we'd almost given up hope of finding you," said her father, and he picked her up and wrapped her snugly in his cloak.

Primrose was nearly asleep by the time they got home. Lady Woodmouse carried her up to her little room and took off her wet clothes. A clean nightie was warming by the fire and a mug of hot acorn coffee had been placed by the bed.

"I'll never ever go out of the field on my own again," Primrose whispered sleepily.

Her mother gave her a kiss and smoothed her pillow.

"Ease your whiskers, rest your paws,
Pies and puddings fill the stores.
Sweetly dream the night away,
Till sunshine brings another day,"

. . . she sang softly, tucking Primrose into her comfy bed.